Mission: Addition

written and illustrated by

Loreen Leedy

Holiday House · New York

For our newest addition,
my niece Deborah Grace

$5+3=8$

$4+1=5$

$2+3=5$

Library of Congress Cataloging-in-Publication Data
Leedy, Loreen.
Mission : addition / by Loreen Leedy.
p.   cm.
Summary: Miss Prime and her animal students explore addition by
finding many examples in the world around them.
ISBN 0-8234-1307-1 (lib. bdg.)
1. Addition—Juvenile literature.   [1. Addition.]   I. Title.
QA115.L445   1997   96-37149   CIP   AC
513.2'11—dc21
ISBN 0-8234-1412-4 (pbk.)

Contents

MISSION: ADDITION

It was a stormy day, and Miss Prime's classroom was dark.

I'm going to show you just the facts— the addition facts.

Suppose you're a detective and you find two fingerprints, then you find three more.

Here's how you write the addition fact with numbers:

2 + 3 = 5

Can you think of something else that might be a clue when you're solving a case?

Footprints?

Okay! What if you see three footprints on the path and two footprints in the flower bed?

Three plus two equals five footprints!

$$3 + 2 = 5$$

Right! Now I have a case for you to solve. Early this morning, somebody ate the cookies in my secret box of chocolate chip cookies.

Look around the room for clues, and when you think you know who did it, report back to me.

BIG CHIP

The numbers you add together are called addends. The answer is the sum.

$$2 + 3 = 5$$
addend   addend   sum

If you change the order of the addends, does it change the sum?

$$3 + 2 = ?$$

See page 32 for the answer.

Having Sum Fun

One afternoon, Ginger and Fay looked inside some boxes in Fay's basement.

It All Adds Up

It was survey day in the classroom.

How many pets without fur or fins do Miss Prime's students have?

I don't have fur or fins.

Neither do I.

Tally's closet was overflowing with his stuff.

18

This lamp is lovely!
It belonged to my great uncle. Six dollars, please.
6
10 +6 16

I've been looking for one of these.
This is your lucky day—that will be three dollars, please.
Woof! I've made nineteen dollars!
3
16 +3 19

What Is Your Problem?

Miss Prime held up a big poster.

Today we're going to invent our own word problems.

For example, how many yellow flowers can you see? How many red ones? How many flowers in all?

yellow ⫽⫽⫽⫽ red ⫽⫽⫽

$$\begin{array}{r} 5 \\ +3 \\ \hline 8 \end{array}$$

Here are the answers: There are five yellow flowers and three red ones, which add up to eight flowers in all.

I knew that.

carrot
||
apple
|||
peach
|
strawberry
卅||
green pepper
|

$$\begin{array}{r} 2 \\ 3 \\ 1 \\ 7 \\ + 1 \\ \hline 14 \end{array}$$

If you add up all the red items shown in the posters, what is the total sum?

That's an easy one.

Maybe so, but can you get the right answer? (It's on page 32.)

It was late morning, and everyone was getting hungry.

You may buy whatever you'd like to eat, but be sure you have enough money to pay for everything you choose.

27

28

This should add up to six. Miss Prime, did you add these up wrong on purpose?
Who, me? Why would I do that?
Salad 3
Dessert 2
Drink + 1
60

Umm . . . this is added up right, but I don't have enough money to pay it.
Oh well, I guess you'll have to stay after school to wash dishes.
Sandwich 4
Sandwich 4
Salad 3
Dessert 2
Dessert 2
Dessert 2
Drink 1
Drink + 1
19

One way to check addition is to simply add up the numbers again to see if the sum is the same.

What is another way to check addition?

Answers

page 8: It doesn't matter in which order you add the addends—the sum will be the same.
$$2 + 3 = 3 + 2$$

page 11:

$$\begin{array}{r} 4 \\ + 12 \\ \hline 16 \end{array} \qquad \begin{array}{r} 11 \\ + 7 \\ \hline 18 \end{array} \qquad \begin{array}{r} 13 \\ + 6 \\ \hline 19 \end{array}$$

page 15: They have nine reptiles and eight birds (no fur or fins on any of those) for a total of seventeen.

$$\begin{array}{r} 9 \\ + 8 \\ \hline 17 \end{array}$$

No fur · No fur or fins · No fins

page 20: Five. (One customer came back twice.)

page 25: Three red flowers, two starfish, three apples, and seven strawberries add up to fifteen red items. $3 + 2 + 3 + 7 = 15$

page 31: Another way to check addition is to subtract an addend from the sum; the result should be the other addend.
$6 + 3 = 9$ check: $9 - 3 = 6$ ✓